PRAISE FOR THE BOOK
Breaking Up With Babel

There is NOBODY like Nikki when it comes to teaching on all things sexuality. Our society is obsessed with this topic and TikTok is shaping this generation's worldview. Is it no wonder they have become the most unhappy one in history? The truth Nikki brings into this space is life changing. Her message is honest yet filled with compassion for the many who have been left broken. There is good news when it comes to our sexuality and it is found in the Bible! Nikki is the biology theology expert, and I have personally watched how people lean in and can't get enough of her teaching. We are so excited she has made her message accessible to everyone through this book because this generation desperately needs to hear it.

– *Cam and Renee Bennett, National Youth Alive Directors, Australia.*

As a former senior pastor, and current leader of the many ACC churches in NSW/ACT, I am constantly looking for ways to empower Christians to engage with anddisciple the next generation. Whether we like it or not, sexuality andrelationships are part of this conversation, and the sexual message in Scripture is only becoming more significant as we connect with the generation outside the walls of our Sunday services. In her new book *Breaking Up with Babel*, Nikki unapologetically takes on the subject of sex, dating and relationships in a way that not only gives Christians confidence in their Bibles but a message of hope and restoration for unbelievers! Nikki offers profound tools for those who want to challenge culture and champion purity, as well as holy hope for the questioning, confused and broken. I cannot recommend this book enough to those who are passionate about reaching their generation in a tangible and powerful way.

– *Paul Bartlett, ACC (Australian Christian Churches) NSW & ACT State President, ACC National, Director for Community Engagement.*

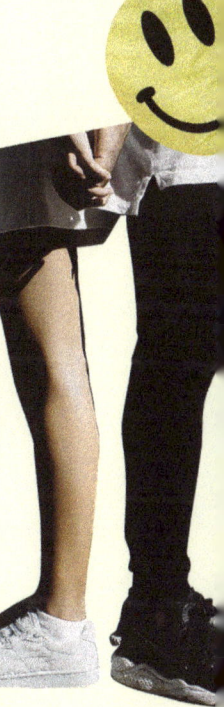

As a senior pastor with a large percentage of youth and young adults, I am conscious of equipping the next generation with biblical truths around sexuality and identity. Nikki's book is a word in season for pastors, youth pastors and leaders, scripture teachers, parents, young adults and youth. Nikki is brilliant and gifted at explaining deep and complex truths in a way that is retainable and relatable to the young modern reader. When it comes to living out Christian values, this book will give you the often unexplained 'why's' behind 'what' we believe in relation to identity and sexuality. I believe this book is going to become a pivotal tool for training the next generation. I highly recommend this book from both a pastoral perspective, and as a mother of three pre-teen children. I am grateful to have it as a resource in my life and ministry.

– *Louise Antonius, Senior Pastor Eastcoast Church, Sydney, ACC NSW & ACT Executive*

INTRODUCTION	IV.
1. IDENTITY: *Filters & Fig Leaves*	1.
2. GENDER: *Mugs & Tea Cups*	7.
3. BOUNDARIES: *Walls & Treasure*	13.
4. SINGLENESS: *Preparing to Win*	19.
5. PLATONIC FRIENDSHIP: *The Friend Zone*	25.
6. DATING: *Becoming the One*	31.
7. TOXIC COUPLES: *The Toxic Couple*	37.
8. HEALTHY COUPLES: *Relationship Goals*	43.
9. SEX, SCIENCE & SCRIPTURE: *The Sexual Gospel*	49.
10. HEALING BROKENESS: *Binding Broken Hearts*	55.
END NOTES	61.
PRAYER APPENDIX	63.
RECOMMENDED RESOURCES	65.
ABOUT THE AUTHOR	67.

INTRODUCTION

WELCOME

Welcome all youth and young adult leaders! [And, in fact, anyone who is involved in the noble and crucial task of discipling young people.] I highly encourage you to return to this topic frequently in your ministry - it will always be relevant, powerful and necessary to walk them through these formative years where they are still shaping their convictions around love, sex, gender and identity.

Many young people are oversaturated with scrolling screens, online dating feeds and deceptive ideologies. If we don't disciple young people around God's view of these topics [because it feels difficult, awkward, intimidating or controversial] then trending culture will swiftly and willingly disciple them instead into unhealthy and destructive ideas.

The flip side? When we do disciple them in the truth of God's Word and the ways of His Kingdom, it becomes one of the most powerful and life-changing ways that Jesus moves and works in their life. Because the sexual worldview of the Bible is a gospel. It's GOOD news. It is a brighter and more hopeful, healthy, fruitful and flourishing worldview than what TikTok and Hinge present to this generation.

HOW TO USE THIS CURRICULUM

This 10 week curriculum runs for the duration of roughly one school term, if taught week to week. The aim is to give you a discipleship framework to plan around, including sermon content, connect group questions and ministry guidance.

The topics correspond to various chapters of my book *Breaking Up with Babel: The Gospel of Sex, Dating and Relating in a Culture of Confusion.* You don't need the book to use this curriculum, although it's recommended.

I know you're probably short on time because you're organising games, fundraising and getting your youth merchandise sorted. So your sermon content is all there for you - just add your own personal stories, testimonies and prayers. There's 4 points for each topic, and you can choose to use one, some, or all of them, for each week.

INTRODUCTION

At the back of this book, you'll notice a Prayer Appendix, with guided prayers to equip you and your team in ministering around certain topics. Feel free to adapt them to your unique context.

DEALING WITH TRIGGERS

If you become aware of abuse or trauma, please follow the child safety protocol of your church. For example, Australian Christian Churches have a "Toward Safe Places" procedure regarding how to respond to those who confide in their youth leaders regarding these issues. Have a conversation with your senior pastor or ministry oversight about how to approach sensitive and confidential situations.

WHY YOU'RE USING THIS CURRICULUM

I want you to know that you have been hand picked for a holy purpose and heavenly assignment to disciple young people through this cultural moment and season of history. The following passage is known as Jeremiah's Calling Narrative - I want you to read it and prophecy it over yourself today:

Jeremiah 1:5-10 "Before I formed you in the womb I knew you, before you were born I set you apart; I appointed you as a prophet to the nations." "Alas, Sovereign Lord," I said, "I do not know how to speak; I am too young." But the Lord said to me, "Do not say, 'I am too young.' You must go to everyone I send you to and say whatever I command you. Do not be afraid of them, for I am with you and will rescue you," declares the Lord. Then the Lord reached out his hand and touched my mouth and said to me, "I have put my words in your mouth. See, today I appoint you over nations and kingdoms to uproot and tear down, to destroy and overthrow, to build and to plant."

Our calling is to pull down the toxic and deceptive ideas that hold young people captive, and build their futures, destinies, and legacies by planting them in the truth of God's Word and the love of their heavenly Father.

You've got this. He's anointed you for it.

Topic Overview

WEEK 1: IDENTITY

SERMON TITLE SUGGESTION: "Filters & Fig Leaves"

SERMON POINTS
* THE BIBLE DEFINES IDENTITY
* THE BLUEPRINTS FOR IDENTITY
* FILTERS & FIG LEAVES
* RESTORED IDENTITY

SCRIPTURES
* Psalm 139:13-16
* Genesis 1:26-28
* Genesis 3:10

MINISTRY TIME
* Prayer for Holy Spirit to reveal or restore Kingdom identity
* Pray for the Spirit of Truth to lead people into truth
* Song suggestion: *Who You Say I Am*, Hillsong Worship, 2018[1]

CONNECT GROUP QUESTIONS
* What things have you personally used to express your identity? [E.g. feelings, ideas, experiences, Scripture]
* Out of the above, which of these is stable, secure and unchanging?
* What words or phrases does the Bible use to describe us? [E.g. beloved, adopted, saints, sheep, stones]
* What does it mean to be conformed to Christ's image?
* How do you become a child of God?

READING FROM BREAKING UP WITH BABEL
* Chapters 1 & 5

ADDITIONAL HELPFUL RESOURCES
* *Affirming God's Image: Addressing the Transgender Question with Science and Scripture* by Dr. J. Alan Branch
* Creation Ministries International: https://creation.com

FILTERS & FIG LEAVES
Sermon Notes

THE BIBLE DEFINES IDENTITY

What is identity? Identity is the answer to the question: Who am I? By dictionary definition, it is the fact of being who one is. Our culture presents identity as something that is fluid and self-determined, driven by our feelings, the community we surround ourselves with, or the ideology we subscribe to. In basic terms: you can define who you are, and that definition can change according to how you feel. But we need something more stable than things like feelings, peers, opinions, and trending ideas to form our identity - because all these things are subject to human failure and fracture.

If our identity is defined by something that is fluid and changeable, then our entire sense of who we are will fall apart as soon as those things fall apart. We need to know who we are even when we have a bad day, our peers have rejected us, or we've failed miserably. The good news is, our identity is not rooted in psychology, but theology. Who we are is not defined by what our feelings say - but what God says. That's why, if we're going to talk about identity, we must start with the Bible as our foundation for truth. People are desperate to know: Who am I? Where did I come from? What's my purpose? And where am I going?

FILTERS & FIG LEAVES
Sermon Notes

THE BLUEPRINTS FOR IDENTITY

We find our answer to this question in the Garden of Eden. Genesis 1:26-28 says,

"God created mankind in his own image, in the image of God he created them; male and female he created them. God blessed them and said to them, "Be fruitful and increase in number; fill the earth and subdue it."

In just 3 verses we discover the blueprint of our identity, involving:

* Loving origins [where did I come from?]

* Destiny [where am I going?]

* Purpose [why am I here?]

* Community [how do I relate to the world?]

Genesis declares that we are not an accident. We are not here by chance. We are intelligently, creatively, lovingly and purposely designed in the image of a loving God. We have a heavenly assignment and God-given purpose that frames our entire life-span and will leave a fingerprint on the earth once we've gone, instilling us with infinite worth, eternal value, unshakeable destiny and daily purpose. Nothing we feel changes this truth. The devil seeks to sabotage our identity so he can sabotage our heavenly assignment. In order to do this, he has to keep us from the revelation of who we are in Christ - he has to assault our identity.

FILTERS & FIG LEAVES
Sermon Notes

FILTERS AND FIG LEAVES

When God created humanity, there was no self-hatred, no shame, no identity confusion, and no hinderance to healthy relationships. Genesis 3 then describes the first time the devil assaulted humanity's identity. He fed them lies that caused them to doubt God, doubt His good intentions, and doubt who He created them to be. When they rejected God's truth, their relationship with God was broken, and they became confused and ashamed. Genesis 3:7 tells us that when the first humans disobeyed God and ate the forbidden fruit, "At that moment their eyes were opened, and they suddenly felt shame at their nakedness. So they sewed fig leaves together to cover themselves."

Ever since then, we have used filters and fig leaves to choose our own identity and make our own rules. But if we don't know God, we don't know who we are. Evolution teaches us that we are a product of chemical chance with no intelligent design or caring Creator. If we don't know where we came from and why we're here, the only thing that remotely makes us feel human or meaningful is our emotions and feelings, so we think these must define my reality, identity and purpose.

But if how we feel determines who we are, then if we fail, we must be a failure. If we feel worthless, we must be worthless. If we feel ugly, we must be ugly. The Bible has an infinitely and eternally more hopeful message of humanity than what TikTok preaches to us! WHO we are is entirely defined by WHOSE we are. We don't have to change our appearance, filter our face or let our feelings rule our life. Our longing for identity is found in being known by the very God who made us uniquely, personally and individually. He knows, as Jesus says, every hair on our head! [Luke 12:7]

FILTERS & FIG LEAVES
Sermon Notes

RESTORED IDENTITY

If you follow our story in Genesis, you'll notice that God sacrificed an animal [Genesis 3:21] in order to make clothing for Adam and Eve. In an unforeseen act of mercy, God used the skin of the unnamed animal to clothe them, and hide their shame. He brought them out of hiding, and instead hid their shame behind the skin of the innocent, who bled and died for them. One day, God would not send an animal. He would send His Son. Jesus Christ is the Innocent One, and his sacrifice covers all our sin, our shame, our brokenness, our confusion, our skewed identity. This is what it means to be made into a "new creation" in 2 Corinthians 5:17. We are given a new nature, and with it, a new name. This name is what will identify us and define who we are.

What is this new identity? We are now called sons and daughters. 2 Corinthians 6:10 says, "I will be a Father to you, and you will be my sons and daughters, says the Lord Almighty." Think about your identity as a son or daughter of your own parents - this reality does not change according to how you, or they, feel. Even when your parents die, you will still be their son or daughter. Even if you're estranged from your parents or hate them, it does't change your status as their child. For the confused, the questioning, the rejected and the broken, the gospel is not a message of transitory identity – but transformational identity!

When we abandon our self-made fig leaves and attempts to self-identify, we receive our God-given identity as a child of God! John 1:12, "But to all who did receive him, who believed in his name, he gave the right to become children of God." God is the perfect Father, who never abandons us, fiercely loves all His children, and desires a personal relationship with you. If you're His child, you'll always be His child. You are cherished and treasured by God, intelligently created by God, made worthy by the blood of God and transformed by the Spirit of God!

WK2

GENDER

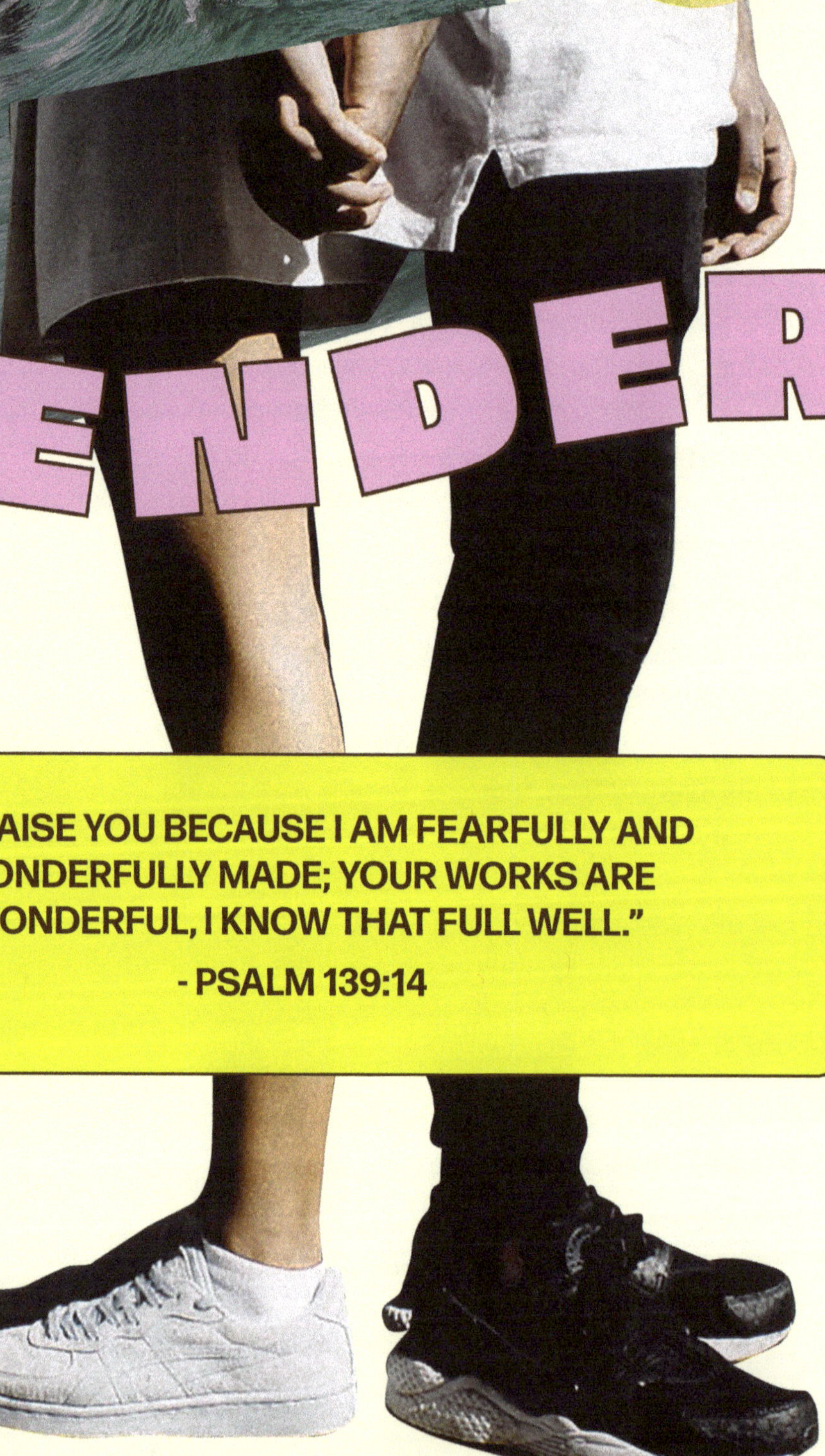

"I PRAISE YOU BECAUSE I AM FEARFULLY AND WONDERFULLY MADE; YOUR WORKS ARE WONDERFUL, I KNOW THAT FULL WELL."
- PSALM 139:14

Topic Overview

WEEK 2: GENDER

SERMON TITLE SUGGESTION: "Mugs & Tea Cups"

SERMON POINTS
* THE LANGUAGE OF LIFE: D.N.A THE BLUEPRINTS FOR IDENTITY
* MUGS & TEA CUPS
* ROBUST AND TENDER SONS
* POWERFUL AND PRECIOUS DAUGHTERS

SCRIPTURES
* Psalm 139:14
* 1 Peter 3:7
* Romans 16:12

MINISTRY TIME
* Prophesy people's identity as sons and daughters of God
* Ask the Holy Spirit to reveal to people what it means to be a child of God
* Song suggestion: *No Longer Slaves,* Bethel Music, 2015[2]

CONNECT GROUP QUESTIONS
* Who are your favourite male and female Bible characters, and why?
* Do you feel content with the way God has made you? Why/why not?
* How can you better hear God's voice for your life and identity?
* Why is your body sacred?
* How can your mind be renewed when it comes to feelings that don't match up with reality?

READING FROM BREAKING UP WITH BABEL
* Chapters 4 & 5

ADDITIONAL HELPFUL RESOURCES
* *Gender Ideology: What Do Christians Need to Know* by Sharon James
* *Mama Bear Apologetics: Empowering Your Kids to Understand and Live Out God's Design* by Hillary Morgan Ferrer & Amy Davidson
* Creation Ministries International: https://creation.com

MUGS & TEA CUPS
Sermon Notes

THE LANGUAGE OF LIFE: D.N.A

The testimony of Scripture declares that although men and women are equal, there is glorious beauty within their differences. These differences of course are primarily determined by something extraordinary called D.N.A. Did you know D.N.A. is the most sophisticated language in the world? It is the very blueprint and language of life. It is by far the densest information storage mechanism in the world. The information in one pin-head of DNA is the equivalent to a pile of books reaching 500x the distance from here to the moon![3] And every single living thing is created from this code of life: D.N.A!

However, language only carries meaning because words demand a speaker. Who is the Speaker of this highly advanced language? Evolutionists argue that D.N.A. is a product of chance, but still have to admit that it is a statistically improbable and mind-bending chance! The probability of the accidental formation of even one functional cell is acknowledged to be worse than 1 in 10^{57800}.[4] However, Christians know humans and cells are no accident of atoms or chemical explosion. The very first recorded action we have in the Bible is the Speaker speaking the language of life. Genesis 1:3 declares, "Then God said…" The Living God chose to use words to create life. D.N.A predetermines our race, gender and age. This is what scientists call "biological determinism", where genetics scientifically predict and predetermine your hair, eye and skin colour. Upon these foundations the science of medicine is built.

MUGS & TEA CUPS
Sermon Notes

MUGS & TEA CUPS

1 Peter 3:7 says, "Husbands, live with your wives in an understanding way, showing honor to the woman as the delicate vessel, since they are heirs with you of the grace of life…"

Let's imagine putting a mug and a fine china teacup next to one another. Both are vessels that by and large do the same thing: they hold liquid. They are completely equal in their potential. They can hold the same amount of boiling hot water and withstand the same amount of heat. They are similar, but not identical, in shape and structure - both have handles to grasp and rounded edges, meaning they are used in the same way. But they're different! Mugs are sturdy and strong, so they can withstand a bit of rough manhandling. Generally speaking, males are like mugs - they're the physically stronger vessel. They're biologically designed with more testosterone and increased muscle mass, which is why it isn't fair to put men and women in the same categories for certain sports.

The fine china teacup, on the other hand, is more delicate. It's refined and admired in a different way. Physiologically, girls are more delicate than boys. Female skin is softer [males have tougher skin.] The female body is softer, since we have less genetic capacity for muscle. Although females of course can be muscular and athletic, soft fat sits on the chest, thighs, and hips more so than males. The fine china is more precious, so Grandma exalts it to a special place called the china cabinet, where it gets extra protection in the cabinet so rough people can't handle it in a way that damages it.

Precious is not a synonym for weak. Precious carries the idea of being cherished and treasured. It is a universal observation that there is a preciousness in women that men do not have. Hollywood attempts to either exploit it, reducing women to sexual objects rather than sacred image-bearers – or encourages girls forfeit or filter those traits and virtues that express their femininity. For the girls who don't view themselves as beautiful, precious or treasured, perhaps it's because we've defined "beauty" by TikTok, instead of Scripture. Girls are precious and beautiful not because of how fit or fashionable they are, but simply by virtue of being female. This is God's heart for girls.

MUGS & TEA CUPS
Sermon Notes

ROBUST AND TENDER SONS

Men and women both have value, dignity, potential and authority - but there is a preciousness to women that requires protecting. Women and children are the most oppressed and violated demographic on the planet, and always have been. God has instilled something in every male [with a bit of help from hormones like testosterone and vasopressin!] to shield that quality from being broken or assaulted. When bombs explode and bullets are flying, there is something special, valiant, chivalrous and protective within men that would rather go to the front line to protect what is precious.

In a world full of violence where women have been assaulted and oppressed, Scripture charges husbands with an astonishing mission to, "...love your wives, just as Christ loved the church. He gave up his life for her" [Ephesians 5:25].

King David [1-2 Samuel] is described as a tender poet but a tough warrior! Males can be robust, tough and protective without sacrificing tenderness, gentleness and emotions.

MUGS & TEA CUPS

Sermon Notes

POWERFUL AND PRECIOUS DAUGHTERS

In Romans 16:12, Paul the Apostle affirms the precious strength of women when he sends greetings to the sisters, Tryphena and Tryphosa. He commends them for being women who "work hard in the Lord." This is a deliberate play on words since their names meant "delicate" [Tryphena] and "dainty" [Tryphosa.] Paul emphasises that despite their outward daintiness, these women were mighty labourers for the gospel and God was powerfully at work through them! Females can be the precious vessel without sacrificing their strength at the same time.

The gospel declares that the same Spirit that lives within Christian men is the same Spirit that lives within Christian women. The Spirit is not somehow diluted or weakened when He resides in the "delicate" female vessel. The work of the Holy Spirit in and through us places dignity upon both genders, right down to every pinhead of D.N.A. We don't have to be the same in order to be powerful. Men and women are the same, yet we are different, and together we bear the image of God!

Topic Overview

WEEK 3: BOUNDARIES

SERMON TITLE SUGGESTION: "Walls & Treasure"

SERMON POINTS
* WHAT'S A BOUNDARY?
* BOUNDARIES COMMUNICATE VALUE
* BOUNDARIES ARE FOR PROTECTION, NOT RESTRICTION
* REBUILDING BROKEN WALLS

SCRIPTURES
* Proverbs 4:23
* Nehemiah 4:6
* Psalm 16:5-8

MINISTRY TIME
* Holy Spirit reveal our broken walls where we have had broken/no boundaries
* Ask Jesus to bring restoration of broken walls
* Song suggestion: *Broken Vessels*, Hillsong Worship, 2014[5]

CONNECT GROUP QUESTIONS
* What are some boundaries that might be helpful in romantic relationships?
* Can you think of a time when you crossed a boundary?
* What were the results? Were they immediate or eventual?
* Are there areas in your life that are vulnerable and unprotected?
* How can you partner with the Holy Spirit to rebuild broken walls in your life?

READING FROM BREAKING UP WITH BABEL
* Chapters 6 & 10

ADDITIONAL HELPFUL RESOURCES
* *Boundaries: When to Say Yes, How to Say No to Take Control of Your Life* by Henry Cloud & John Townsend
* *Keep Your Love On: Connection, Communication & Boundaries* by Danny Silk

WALLS & TREASURE
Sermon Notes

WHAT'S A BOUNDARY?

Our physical heart is a vessel with tubes that pumps oxygenated blood through our whole body, giving life to all our major organs. Whatever is in the heart will end up in all other parts of our body, because the heart is intrinsically connected to every part of our physical being. In the same way, Proverbs 4:23 tells us our spiritual heart is a vessel, from which all our behaviour and decisions flow. This means that whatever is in our heart will eventually flow into every area of our life, especially our relationships! Because our heart is so valuable, the Bible tells us to guard our heart as a precious vessel and ensure only healthy, wholesome, pure things are filling it.

How do we guard something? Well, the same way we guard anything valuable in this world: with boundaries! What is a boundary? Boundaries are indicators that bring identification and protection. For example, the fence in my yard is a boundary that identifies my property and protects it from intruders. The word "no" is a boundary that can identify my values and protect me from being violated. My bank PIN is a boundary that identifies my bank account and keeps you from robbing it!

WALLS & TREASURE
Sermon Notes

BOUNDARIES COMMUNICATE VALUE

You'll notice that things of little value are often not protected with boundaries. No one needs to put an electric fence around a garbage bin or place a 10 cent coin in a vault. So if you want to spot a boundary, just look for something really expensive! Picture a giant jewel in the centre of the museum. It's guarded by ropes, lasers, security cameras, and security guards. Basically, nobody can get to the jewel because it's surrounded by boundaries! Boundaries therefore send the message: "this is valuable, and only the privileged can touch it." The privileged person who gets to handle the jewel is the person who can be trusted with it: they won't steal it or sell it for their own selfish gain. They won't damage it in their clumsiness or carelessness.

For this reason, the issue of boundaries is one of self-worth. We will only guard ourselves to the degree that we value ourselves. Have you noticed that the people who don't value themselves tend to have very little boundaries? If you don't think yourself worthy of blessing and protection, you won't put in the boundaries that lead to it. We won't protect our bodies if we don't respect our bodies. We won't put boundaries around our sexuality if we don't regard it as something precious for a purpose. We won't put boundaries in our relationships if we don't value ourselves, or the other person.

It's interesting that we exert so much protection over objects of value like diamonds, money, and even our iPhones - but not nearly so much with the pinnacle of all created things: ourselves. You can only trust someone with your entire self [body, mind, and heart] if they have laid down their lives for you in marriage. This is the "privileged person" who gets to hold the prized gem of our sexuality, having proven their integrity and trustworthiness. In the meantime, we will put appropriate boundaries in place to protect something so valuable and vulnerable.

WALLS & TREASURE
Sermon Notes

BOUNDARIES ARE FOR PROTECTION, NOT RESTRICTION

One of the most noticeable boundaries in the Bible was walls. The city of Jerusalem had sturdy walls around it, and they were the structure that stood between enemy attacks and God's people. Walls were basically big boundaries that provided peace and wellbeing for the people who lived inside them. They even became a metaphor for salvation; not just physically from military enemies, but spiritually. Isaiah 60:18 says, "You shall call your walls salvation and your gates praise."

To put it plainly, the boundaries around the city became blessings to the people within them. And it is no different to the boundaries we put in our own relationships! Relationships lacking good boundaries give selfish people easy access. This is what we call being 'used' by someone, and a user is of course a selfish person, even if they seem friendly. They come in, take what they want, and they leave. Remember the walls around Jerusalem weren't for restriction to trap people in, they were for protection to keep intruders out. So let's think about building boundaries in our relationships the way God's people treasured their walls.

WALLS & TREASURE
Sermon Notes

REBUILDING BROKEN BOUNDARIES

A city without walls opens people up to violation and brokenness, and so does a relationship without boundaries. In the Bible, God's people were defeated because they threw the "Boundary Book" [Bible!] out the window and tried to play by their own rules. They sacrificed their protection and were attacked by enemy nations who robbed their dignity and oppressed them. These enemies set fire to Israel's walls and broke them down.

Aren't you thankful that there is an entire book in your Bible dedicated to rebuilding walls? The book of Nehemiah tells the story of God helping His people rebuild the walls, taking away their national shame and restoring their honour, authority and strength - and when it comes to boundaries, God still does this! Imagine if we protected our sexuality, body, mind, and heart with strong, healthy boundaries so that by the time we stepped up to the wedding altar, we knew the person standing opposite us was trustworthy to be granted access to all of us. What a celebration that would be!

Maybe your walls have never crumbled – good for you! Keep them intact, and continue to be brave enough to say, "This far and no further, thanks." But for those who have let their walls crumble, Nehemiah's story fills us with hope for restoration. The Enemy knows that rebuilding the walls leads to blessing. They help identify and define us. They restore our honour, authority and strength. They protect our values, virtues and purity. If you're someone who has lacked boundaries in your relationships up until this point, there is absolutely nothing stopping you from picking up your building tools and starting today. Everyone can enjoy the blessings that grow inside boundaries. If we have broken down walls, Jesus is faithful to rebuild and restore, making us strong and secure again.

Topic Overview

WEEK 4: SINGLENESS

SERMON TITLE SUGGESTION: "Preparing to Win"

SERMON POINTS
* PREPARING TO WIN
* BUILDING BOUNDARIES
* A HOPE AND A FUTURE

SCRIPTURES
* 1 Timothy 4:8
* 1 Corinthians 7:7
* Jeremiah 29:11

MINISTRY TIME
* Pray for Jesus to give people a vision and hope for their future
* Ask the Holy Spirit to illuminate friends who can champion their purity and help them towards that future
* Song suggestion: *Hindsight,* Hillsong Young and Free, 2018[6]

CONNECT GROUP QUESTIONS
* Why is singleness so important?
* How can you receive the "gift" that comes from singleness?
* What might be God's vision for your future when it comes to family, marriage and relationships?
* Who are your friends who can support and champion this vision?
* Who is a good example or model of healthy marriage in your life?

READING FROM BREAKING UP WITH BABEL
* Chapter 8

ADDITIONAL HELPFUL RESOURCES
* *The New Rules For Love, Sex, and Dating* by Andy Stanley
* *Single, Dating, Engaged, Married: Navigating Life and Love in the Modern Age* by Ben Stuart

PREPARING TO WIN
Sermon Notes

PREPARING TO WIN

I've never met a young person who said, "I can't wait to get married 3 or 4 times." Deep down we desire to succeed in our future marriage, relationships and families. But if we truly want to succeed and flourish in something, we go to the effort [and sacrifice] to prepare ourselves. Long distance runners might desire to win the gold, but that desire is redundant if they don't actually prepare to win by consistent training! It's one thing to sign up for a race, but it's an entirely other thing to prepare for it. 1 Timothy 4:8 says, "Physical training is good, but training for godliness is much better, promising benefits in this life and in the life to come."

Singleness is the most vital season of your life when it comes to preparing for marriage. It affords us the time to allow God to develop our mindsets, values, lifestyle and friendships. Since they don't hand out magical discipline dust with our wedding certificate, learning self-control and sacrifice is crucial prior to marriage, because it is still needed once you're in it! In this way, we prepare to actually keep the promises we will make one day to that special person at the altar.

PREPARING TO WIN
Sermon Notes

BUILDING BOUNDARIES

Singleness is the prime time to learn about boundaries and set them firmly in place before our hormones come in and hijack the wheel. Let's explore 4 types of boundaries we can build into our lives during this season of singleness:

PHYSICAL BOUNDARIES

The Bible tells us that crossing sexual boundaries prior to marriage is a sin that inevitably robs both parties of sexual blessing, but it's also helpful to remember that even a long hug triggers the trust-circuits in a female brain - whether a man has earned her trust or not! Yes, we must take care who we envelop in intimate hugs![7] Knowing where to draw the line is about setting you both up for success. Rather than asking, "How far is too far?" a better question to ask is, "What completely and wholeheartedly honours and esteems this person? How can I protect this person's heart? How can I safeguard their body and soul?"

SOCIAL BOUNDARIES

It's human nature to stumble when we don't have the accountability of other people's eyeballs! This is why God sets us in community and family. Quite simply, we need one another. When it comes to dating, hanging out in groups is a great way to build trust and free us from the pressure of getting to know someone in an exclusively romantic environment. Besides, how someone treats others is a foretaste of how they'll one day treat you once the honeymoon period wears off and the stresses of life kick in! Dating in isolation robs us of the wisdom we need to navigate this enjoyable but intoxicating world of romance. We need people [Christian friends, leaders and parents] to help us make good choices because when we're attracted to someone, no matter how wise we think we are, we will rarely make an objective decision. Proverbs 27:6 might sting a little, but it could save us from some seriously creepy or toxic people: "Wounds from a sincere friend are better than many kisses from an enemy."

PREPARING TO WIN
Sermon Notes

MENTAL BOUNDARIES

Guard your thought life - because according to Romans 12:2, the mind is so powerful that it is the launchpad for our transformation! If our thoughts have such power to change our lives, we'd better protect them. Rather than letting our feelings rule our thought life, we need to put boundaries around our thinking and essentially tell our thoughts where to go. If we fantasise or meditate obsessively on someone, we create an unhealthy mental attachment and feel a mental void if the relationship ends. It's also a good idea to have boundaries around what kind of music we listen to, books we read, media we watch and feeds we scroll. Listening to the kind of music that sexualises people or watching movies that promote lust is not going to produce a wholesome thought life. The reason our thoughts matter, is because according to Jesus, thoughts lead to actions [Matthew 5:27]. Philippians 4:8 is a powerful boundary: "Fix your thoughts on what is true, and honourable, and right, and pure, and lovely, and admirable. Think about things that are excellent and worthy of praise."

SPIRITUAL BOUNDARIES

2 Corinthians 6:14 says, "Do not be yoked together with unbelievers." The word "yoke" refers to the Old Testament law that forbids hitching two animals of different species together when they were ploughing. For example, if you yoked a donkey and an ox together, they'd go different speeds and different directions. Yoking them together would set them both up for strife and failure, which is unfair to both parties. Paul is telling us that yoking our lives with someone who isn't a believer is unfair and unwise. It will usually lead to one of two things: we'll compromise and go in their direction or we'll impose behaviour modification on them to drag them in our direction. Neither option sets us up for spiritual peace and harmony. When the time is right, yoke yourself to someone in the same Kingdom as you. We don't necessarily need to share the same hobbies and taste in coffee, but our lives need to be orientating around the same faith, values, and headed in the same direction.

PREPARING TO WIN
Sermon Notes

THE GIFT OF SINGLENESS

1 Corinthians 7:7 says, "God gives the gift of the single life to some, the gift of the married life to others" [MSG].

Being single is a gift from God during which something special is to be accomplished. There's nothing wrong with desiring companionship and romance, but many young people rush through their season of singleness like it's a disease they need to rid themselves of. The things that could be accomplished in that season of singleness can be forgone on a series of fruitless & destructive relationships. Instead of asking, "How do I become un-single?" as we swipe left and right on dating profiles, maybe we should look up, and ask, "God, what do you want to do in and through me as a single person?"

King Solomon missed his calling because he had a taste for foreign women and married 700 of them! Don't waste this season - God seeks to build something within us during our singleness that He simply cannot do once we're attached to someone. It's a great time for study, service, travel, developing in God and your giftings, figuring out who you are and your purpose. The Holy Spirit is our ever-present Friend to prepare us, strengthen us, keep us accountable and guide us as we spend our single years laying rock solid foundations for a future filled with hope.

Jeremiah 29:11 "For I know the plans I have for you," says the Lord. "They are plans for good and not for disaster, to give you a future and a hope."

WK5

PLATONIC FRIENDSHIP

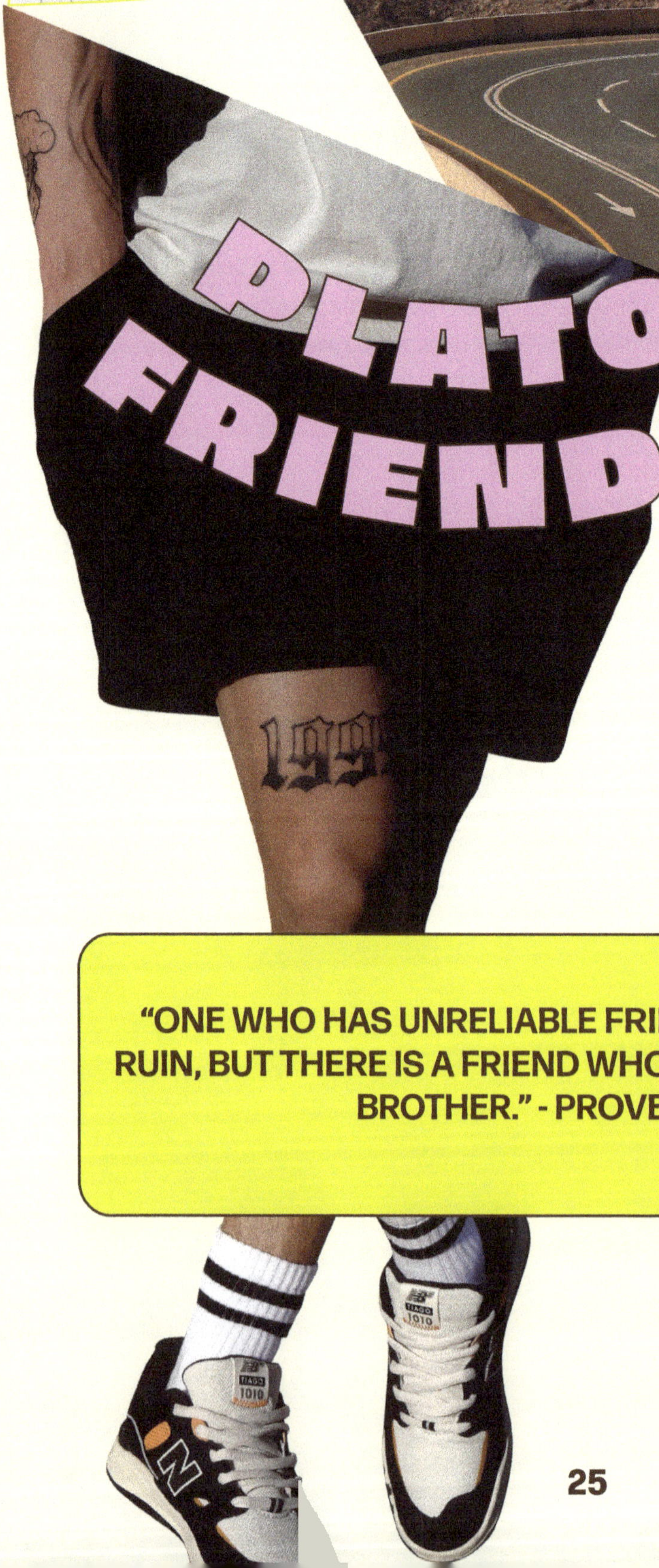

> "ONE WHO HAS UNRELIABLE FRIENDS SOON COMES TO RUIN, BUT THERE IS A FRIEND WHO STICKS CLOSER THAN A BROTHER." - PROVERBS 18:24

Topic Overview

WEEK 5: PLATONIC FRIENDSHIP

SERMON TITLE SUGGESTION: "The Friend Zone"

SERMON POINTS
* LET'S (NOT) GET PHYSICAL
* MATES BEFORE DATES
* THE FRIEND ZONE
* KEEP GROWING

SCRIPTURES
* Proverbs 18:24
* Genesis 11:1-4
* Matthew 7:24-27

MINISTRY TIME
* Give opportunity for people to commit to a fresh start
* Pray for healing over broken homes and families
* Song suggestion: *Build My Life,* Pat Barrett, 2018[8]

CONNECT GROUP QUESTIONS
* Have you ever felt vulnerable or regretful after sharing too much information with someone?
* What signs might you see or feel that tell you a relationship is premature?
* Who gets the most of your quality time? Do you need to rearrange your priorities a little?
* How could a new relationship potentially crowd out the God-seed in you?
* Out of the 4 types of boundaries listed, which one needs most of your attention today?

READING FROM BREAKING UP WITH BABEL
* Chapters 6 & 10

ADDITIONAL HELPFUL RESOURCES
* *Moral Revolution: The Naked Truth About Sexual Purity* by Jason Vallotton and Kris Vallotton
* *Dating Delilah* by Judah Smith

THE FRIEND ZONE
Sermon Notes

LET'S [NOT] GET PHYSICAL

The foundation of every fruitful relationship is friendship. Learning how to interact with the opposite sex in a healthy, platonic way paves the path for healthy romance in the future. When the friendship stage is shortened or skipped, the relationship is very much about the physical side of things. So many gauge their relationship by the 'lust level' [how strong their feelings are or how far they go physically.] Feelings and physical contact aren't a gauge for a relationship. We need chemistry to fall in love, but we need something more to stay in love. True, lasting love requires choice, commitment, self control, discipline, sacrifice. It requires more than feelings and attraction - and we need to slow down in order to prepare ourselves for the "more".

Intimacy is wonderful, but it has a special place and timing attached to it. It's important to remember that intimacy isn't just sexual, it's emotional too. You can sense if two people have a level of intimacy by the way they connect and interact. While friendship is a 'side-by-side' thing, intimacy is a 'face-to-face' thing. Getting too close too soon can lead to exclusivity, and that's a one-way formula to kill your social [and spiritual] life. Immediately pairing off with someone sets you up for premature intimacy. Let's take it slow.

THE FRIEND ZONE
Sermon Notes

MATES BEFORE DATES

And by mates, we're talking about the Aussie slang term for friends [not the definition for breeding.] Friendship is inclusive, but often we see couples drawn into exclusivity and isolation. Have you ever watched a friend start dating someone, and suddenly you never see them anymore? They're drawn away from friends into the exclusive company of their partner, but when that relationship ends, they often find themselves isolated because their friendships have withered. Why did they wither? They didn't sow time, energy and care into their friendships - because they were attempting to get all their needs met by one romantic relationship.

Here's the thing though: we're created for community, not exclusivity. If you attempt to get all your needs met by one person, they eventually become your "god". They've taken the role that they simply cannot fill. Jesus is the only Saviour and ultimate need-meeter! The beauty of friendships is that you can have lots of them - you can pursue friendship with loads of people and learn how they interact with yourself and others. The freedom of friendship allows us to interact in the context of fun and loving community and sets us up to be secure, healthy, balanced people.

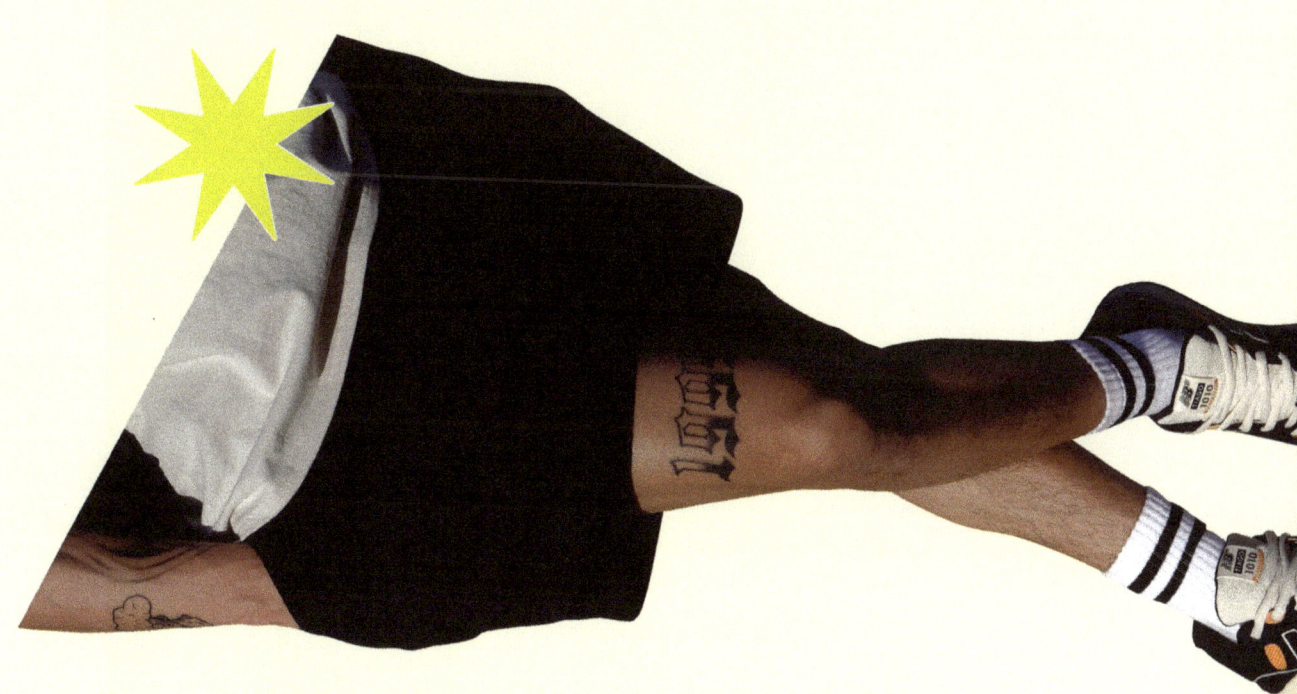

THE FRIEND ZONE
Sermon Notes

THE FRIEND ZONE

The good news is, we don't need to prepare for marriage via a string of painful break-ups. Contrary to the advocates for try-before-you-buy dating, people are not platforms upon which we must train for marriage. Friendship is. Can we build friendship with someone we have romantic feelings for? Of course! You can be friends with all kinds of people. Befriending someone, and eventually committing to them, is how you love someone well. It's an intention to get to know somebody with a desire for a greater commitment in mind down the track - within the safe boundaries of friendship. That "greater commitment down the track" is marriage.

If you are nowhere near the age where you can actually get married, dating people isn't really on your radar. However, learning to do platonic friendship with the opposite sex healthily is! Boring? No - it's vital. It's the first foundation to build upon for the future. How do we define platonic? It's means no sexual, romantic or emotional expectations. You don't belong to each other; you belong to God and your parents. You'd be surprised how many young people struggle to have good-clean-fun with the opposite sex. Learning how to interact with the opposite sex in a healthy, platonic way paves the path for healthy romance in the future.

THE FRIEND ZONE
Sermon Notes

KEEP GROWING

One of the best strategies the devil uses to stop new Christians from growing in Christ is to stir up a romance in the early stages of their development. Character growth, academic growth and spiritual growth are often put on hold by a premature romance. Believe it or not, there are higher priorities for a new believer than dating! If you're new in your relationship with Jesus, this season is for growing and flourishing in your relationship with Him, not to rush into one with someone else. At the end of the day, it's our relationship with Jesus alone that will satisfy our heart. Seek Him first and all else with fall into place [Matthew 6:33].

When your relationship with Him is healthy and flourishing, your other relationships will grow and flourish also. Besides, if we learn to be a good friend now, we'll make a better spouse later. One day when we're married and the honeymoon stage is over, we will treat our spouse in a similar way that we treat our friends. Whether or not we learned sacrificial love, selflessness, honour and integrity in our single years will come to light. The Bible doesn't teach us how to date someone – it teaches us how to love someone. And we can love anyone with a sacrificial, friendship love!

WK6

DATING

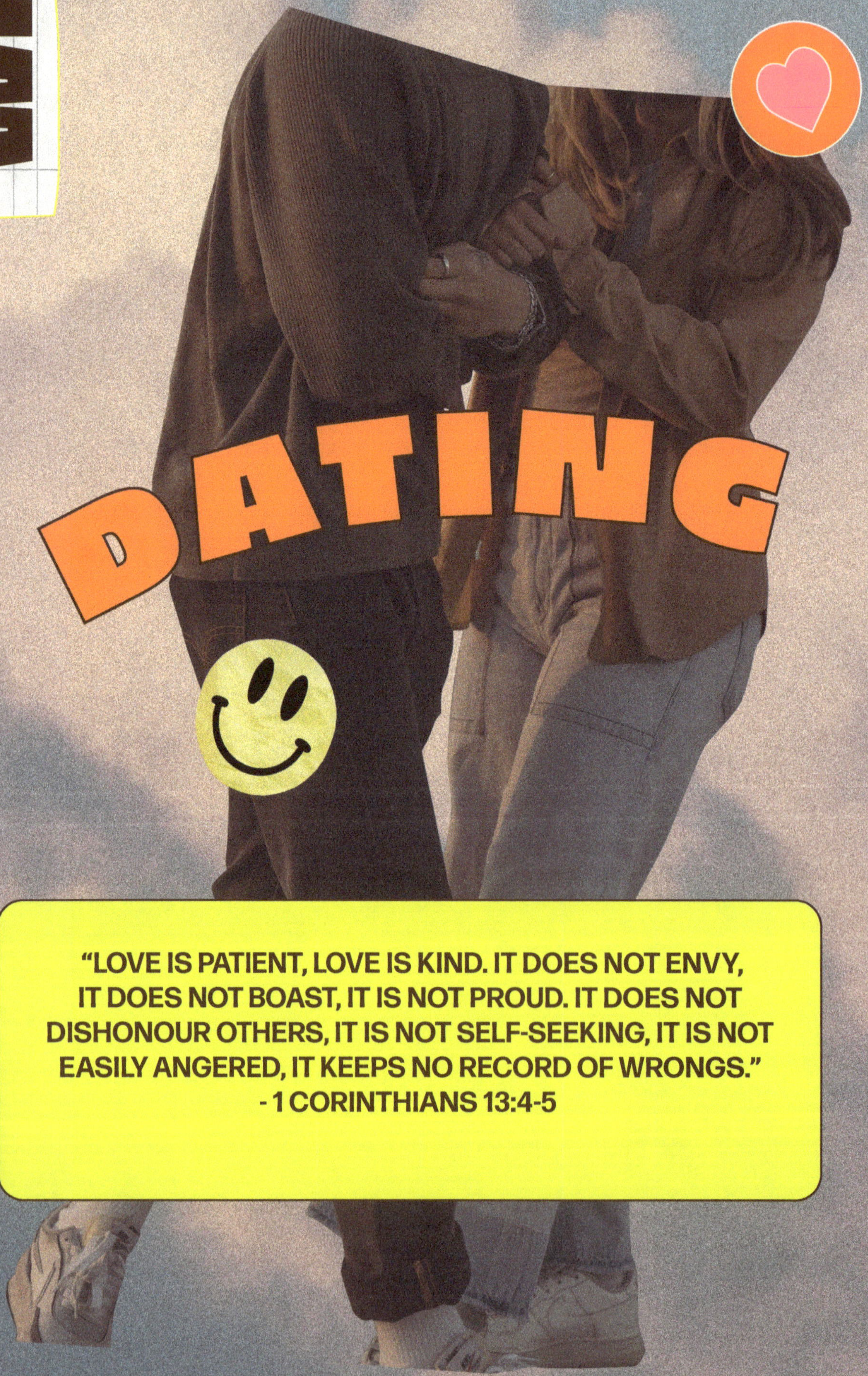

"LOVE IS PATIENT, LOVE IS KIND. IT DOES NOT ENVY, IT DOES NOT BOAST, IT IS NOT PROUD. IT DOES NOT DISHONOUR OTHERS, IT IS NOT SELF-SEEKING, IT IS NOT EASILY ANGERED, IT KEEPS NO RECORD OF WRONGS."
- 1 CORINTHIANS 13:4-5

Topic Overview

WEEK 6: DATING

SERMON TITLE SUGGESTION: "Becoming the One"

SERMON POINTS
* DEFINING DATING
* THE MYTH OF SOUL MATES
* BECOMING THE ONE
* DIGITAL DATING

SCRIPTURES
* Proverbs 18:24
* 1 Corinthians 13:4-5
* Isaiah 55:11

MINISTRY TIME
* Give opportunity for repentance and surrender of relationships
* Pray for encounters with the love of God
* Song suggestion: *Pieces*, Bethel Music, 2016[9]

CONNECT GROUP QUESTIONS
* What is dating? How would you articulate it into 1-2 sentences?
* What are some unhelpful ways dating is presented in movies and media?
* What are some attitudes towards relationships & dating that you need to change?
* Describe your ideal marriage partner - values, attributes, beliefs, passions
* How many of those things can you see in your own life?

READING FROM BREAKING UP WITH BABEL
* Chapters 4 & 7

ADDITIONAL HELPFUL RESOURCES
* *Single, Dating, Engaged, Married: Navigating Life and Love in the Modern Age* by Ben Stuart
* *Boundaries in Dating: How Healthy Choices Grow Healthy Relationships* by Henry Cloud & John Townsend
* *The New Rules For Love, Sex, and Dating* by Andy Stanley

BECOMING THE ONE
Sermon Notes

DEFINING DATING

I don't know if you've noticed, but there is no dating chapter in the Bible. There's a love chapter [1 Corinthians 13]. The Bible certainly talks about relationship, betrothal, and even friendship ... but not dating! "Dating" is a category that we've created between singleness and engagement that didn't exist in the biblical era. So if dating isn't in the Bible, how do I know if it's even biblical? Just because an activity isn't specifically in the Bible, it doesn't mean that Scripture doesn't guide us in how to approach it.

The question should not be, "Is dating biblical?" but rather, "Is my dating biblical?"[10] I should ask the same question of any activities I participate in that aren't specifically in the Bible. Is my driving biblical? Am I getting road rage and cutting people off, or am I taking care to drive responsibly and patiently? Dating is simply the modern label we use for the process of proving you are trustworthy. Trustworthy to what? To marry. This takes time [experiencing life together], training [growing in maturity and learning how to steward someone's heart] and interviews [getting to know one another through observation and conversation.] If you're not anywhere near the age to get married, this is a great time to be laying your friendship foundations.

BECOMING THE ONE
Sermon Notes

THE MYTH OF SOUL MATES

Hollywood's idea of meeting our "soul mate" puts unnecessary pressure on dating. The soul mate issue is really a wrestle between God's sovereignty and our freewill. Does God in His sovereignty nail down one person for us to marry or does He let us choose anyone we want? This idea that there is one "Soul-Mate" out there floating around who we are destined to meet and marry is problematic because it can help justify affairs and divorce. If we hit a snag in our marriage and suddenly meet someone else who appears to tick all our boxes [and triggers all our hormones] we can say, "I think I married the wrong person. Perhaps this person is my soul mate."

The idea of a soul mate actually comes from Greek mythology, which believes you have half a soul and the other half of your soul is in another person somewhere out there.[11] Therefore, you have to find each other and when you do you become one whole person. However, the Bible says God made us unmistakably whole and only He can bring us to wholeness when we're broken. God doesn't make our choices, He shapes our choices. Ever since the He put the Tree of Knowledge in the Garden [Genesis 2:17] God has allowed us the gift of choice. True love is not defined by the level of attraction, amount of common ground we share, or even the burning passion we feel. True love is when people choose to love each other. Day after day. Who we elect as our marriage partner for life becomes "The One" at the altar. We better count the cost and ensure it's a wise decision before we make a life commitment!

BECOMING THE ONE
Sermon Notes

BECOMING THE ONE

The Bible might not use the language of dating, romance, boyfriends or girlfriends, but it most certainly does deal with our relationships. Scripture doesn't say a whole lot about "how to find a great spouse" or "how to have the perfect first date". Because while dating apps promise to help me FIND a great person, the Word of God teaches me how to BE a great person. And this timeless-and-tried Scripture is much more concerned with who we are becoming than who we are finding.

The common denominator of all your relationships, whether it's marriage, friendships, siblings, parents, teachers or pastors: is you. So what if we switched our search from Finding The One and instead let the Word form us into Becoming The One? One who is a loving, honouring, forgiving, even-tempered, others-orientated, authentic, on-mission, on-fire-for-Jesus kind of person. The kind of person we ourselves might want to marry... and see what kind of people Jesus brings into our lives, in His perfect divine timing.

✳✳✳✳

BECOMING THE ONE
Sermon Notes

DIGITAL DATING

Jesus didn't date or have an iPhone, so like anything that isn't illegal or specifically unbiblical, we need to consider what we use online dating for and what appetite it feeds. Digital apps feed our appetites for speed, accelerating the natural pace of a relationship. When the pace quickens, natural stages of organic relationship tend to get skipped. Dating profiles groom us to judge potential partners based on minimal info and appearance, instead of virtues and character. Face-to-face experience is the only way to discover WHO someone is, rather than facts ABOUT them.

Dating apps also provide us with way more romantic options than we could possibly date in real life. We have no choice but to develop a process of elimination to sift through all the prospects, and usually that process is a reflection of social media itself: shallow and erratic. Romantic consumerism can set in, imagining there's always a better option if we pull the refresh button one more time. Loving people sincerely and intelligently is something that glorifies God. If we're feeling ambiguous about dating, it's worth asking ourselves whether our relationship is doing that. Am I loving intelligently, or am I playing with their feelings? Is my interaction with that person glorifying God or is it something that belongs on a Netflix drama? Am I attracting people to Jesus or distracting them?

If we're unsure, 1 Corinthians 13:4-5 provides some solid relationship theology to help us find an answer: "Love is patient, love is kind. It does not envy, it does not boast, it is not proud. It does not dishonour others, it is not self-seeking, it is not easily angered, it keeps no record of wrongs." Whether we call it dating, courting, or the friend zone, if we apply 1 Corinthians 13 to our relationship approach, we won't be disappointed. And while dating apps rarely seem to come good on all their promises, the Word of God never returns void [Isaiah 55:11].

Topic Overview

WEEK 7: TOXIC COUPLES

SERMON TITLE SUGGESTION: "The Toxic Couple: Samson & Delilah"

SERMON POINTS
* TOXIC COUPLES
* ATTRACTION BLINDS US
* SAMSON'S SECOND CHANCE
* BREAKING UP WITH DELILAH

SCRIPTURES
* Judges 16:4-28
* Romans 2:4
* Matthew 5:8

MINISTRY TIME
* Pray for healing from heartbreak and painful break ups
* Pray for freedom from toxic relationships
* Give opportunity for repentance and restoration of pure hearts
* Song suggestion: *Promises Never Fail,* Bethel Music, 2019[12]

CONNECT GROUP QUESTIONS
* Have you ever fallen for someone, knowing they weren't good for you?
* What kind of people, situations or activities make you feel distant from God?
* How would it feel to be betrayed by someone you trusted?
* What is the difference between love and lust?
* How can you be lead by Jesus instead of lust or attraction?

READING FROM BREAKING UP WITH BABEL
* Chapters 7 & 9

ADDITIONAL HELPFUL RESOURCES
* *Dating Delilah* by Judah Smith
* *The New Rules For Love, Sex, and Dating* by Andy Stanley

THE TOXIC COUPLE
Sermon Notes

TOXIC COUPLES

You know that couple who fight constantly, break up and make up, and while everyone else around them can see that the relationship is toxic, they themselves are totally blind to it? Well, there's a couple in the Bible just like this: Samson and Delilah. Samson's story actually begins with his parents [as does yours!] God tells them Samson is called to lead his nation into glorious Kingdom victory. God gives him a special strength to carry out this calling; a supernatural power that lay in his hair, which was never to be cut. But "some time later he fell in love with Delilah" [Judges 16:1].

Firstly, a few verses before this, he was in bed with a prostitute! One chapter before this, a woman from a tribe he was forbidden to marry into, "caught his eyes". Wouldn't it be better if there was a verse thrown in there reading, "And Samson got healed of all his lust issues, and some time later, he fell in love with Delilah." But that's not the way the story goes. If we're taking notes from Samson, being "in love" with someone does not necessarily mean we should be with them! It takes hormones to fall in love. Attraction. Emotion. Being "in love" does not make it right, godly, or destiny. In this case, it was the opposite! This is not a love story - it's a lust story! Lust is driven by the uncontrolled desire to satisfy the self outside of God's boundaries and will. And just like Samson, it usually begins with the eyes. What, or who, we look at will captivate our heart and eventually our body [our decision, behaviour and actions] will shortly follow suit!

THE TOXIC COUPLE
Sermon Notes

ATTRACTION BLINDS US

Most of us read Samson and Delilah's story and are frustrated by their inability to see their own dysfunction. Delilah is lying to Samson in order to take advantage of him. She uses their unhealthy connection and her sexuality to put Samson in a vulnerable position, where he could be taken advantage of. She quite literally "lulls him to sleep" on her lap, and he has also fallen asleep to God's voice, wisdom, and guidance in his life [Judges 16:13]. Samson is constantly lying to Delilah, because he doesn't trust her.

What's with this guy? Why on earth would you stay with someone when it's so obvious they don't have your best intentions at heart? Delilah's selfish manipulation may be easy for us to see, but when you're the one in the relationship, everything becomes complex and twisted. When we're attracted to someone, our brain releases neurochemicals that dilute the other person's faults and magnifies their favourable traits. The butterflies, the hormones, the emotions, the attraction – they intoxicate us, blurring our vision, making it difficult to make rational, objective decisions.

It's actually a phenomenon that happens to our brain called "focalism" which takes place in any situation filled with tension or emotion [especially romantic situations!] Focalism is where we focus on one infatuating thing whilst conveniently excluding all the other facts.[13] In other words, attraction distorts reality! In fact, we can become blind to the reality around us. The power of attraction is potent and potentially dangerous if misused and abused in an unsafe relationship. That's why instead of building the relationship upon the emotions we feel, we must build upon the reality we know. Look at someone's character and fruitfulness over their fashion sense and social media feeds.

THE TOXIC COUPLE
Sermon Notes

SAMSON'S SECOND CHANCE

Judges 16:21 tells us that Samson's enemy, the Philistines, used his toxic relationship with Delilah to trap him, gouge his eyes out, and cut off his hair. Ok - this is set in ancient times, so eye-gouging was more of a common thing - albeit still devastating! But there's a spiritual principle here: Samson's relationship with Delilah ended in blindness, physically and spiritually. How many of us have been in a relationship that blinds us? People become so consumed in their relationship dynamics that they no longer pay attention to God, their friends, their family or their leaders.

Samson forsook his parents [they wanted him to be faithful to his calling but he constantly rebelled], his people [he was supposed to be leading the Israelites into victory, not fooling around with a foreign girl!] and his God [he took advantage of God's gracious gift of strength by using it for the wrong reasons.] But there's hope in this grisly story! Our hope is in Judges 16:22, "But before long, his hair began to grow back." Samson crossed so many lines in disobedience to God - surely God should transfer his destiny to someone more trustworthy to carry out the calling?

Yet God in His grace didn't take away the special gift [of strength] He had granted Samson. Samson's anointing lay in his hair. They cut his hair off, and he [seemingly] lost his gift. However, God has designed hair to grow back. And with it: Samson's gift grew back. Samson's anointing grew back. Samson's calling grew back. Nothing is lost in God - Samson is one of the most sexually broken and messed up guys in the Bible. Yet even in all his failures God still called him, used him and gifted him!

THE TOXIC COUPLE
Sermon Notes

BREAKING UP WITH DELILAH

Samson's story ends in repentance. He cries out to God, finally choosing to use his gift of strength for the reason God gave it to him: for the sake of others. His final moment will be a deeply sacrificial act that fulfils his destiny to bring freedom and salvation to his people [Judges 16:28-29]. Repentance means we break up with the world's way of thinking, and turn to God in agreement and surrender. Romans 2:4 reminds us that repentance is the way back to hope, healing and wholeness: "Don't you see how wonderfully kind, tolerant, and patient God is with you? Does this mean nothing to you? Can't you see that his kindness is intended to turn you from your sin?"

We may have struck out in a failed relationship or stumbled into sexual or emotional sin. Maybe you relate to Samson, with lust issues, relational blindness, or outright disobedience to God and your parents. Or maybe you find yourself more in Delilah - manipulative, using your looks, body and emotions to get what you want. Or maybe you relate to none of these characters and never want to! Either way, know this: the calling remains. The love of God remains. The anointing on your life remains. He doesn't take it away, simply because you've strayed. You may have made mistakes, and lost your way - but God has designed your destiny to grow back. He has designed His mercies to grow back every morning. You can start fresh and do it the right way [God's way] no matter where you find yourself in this story. If you cry out to God like Samson, He will give you a supernatural strength to walk the path to purity and wholeness.

"Blessed are the pure in heart, for they will see God" [Matthew 5:8].

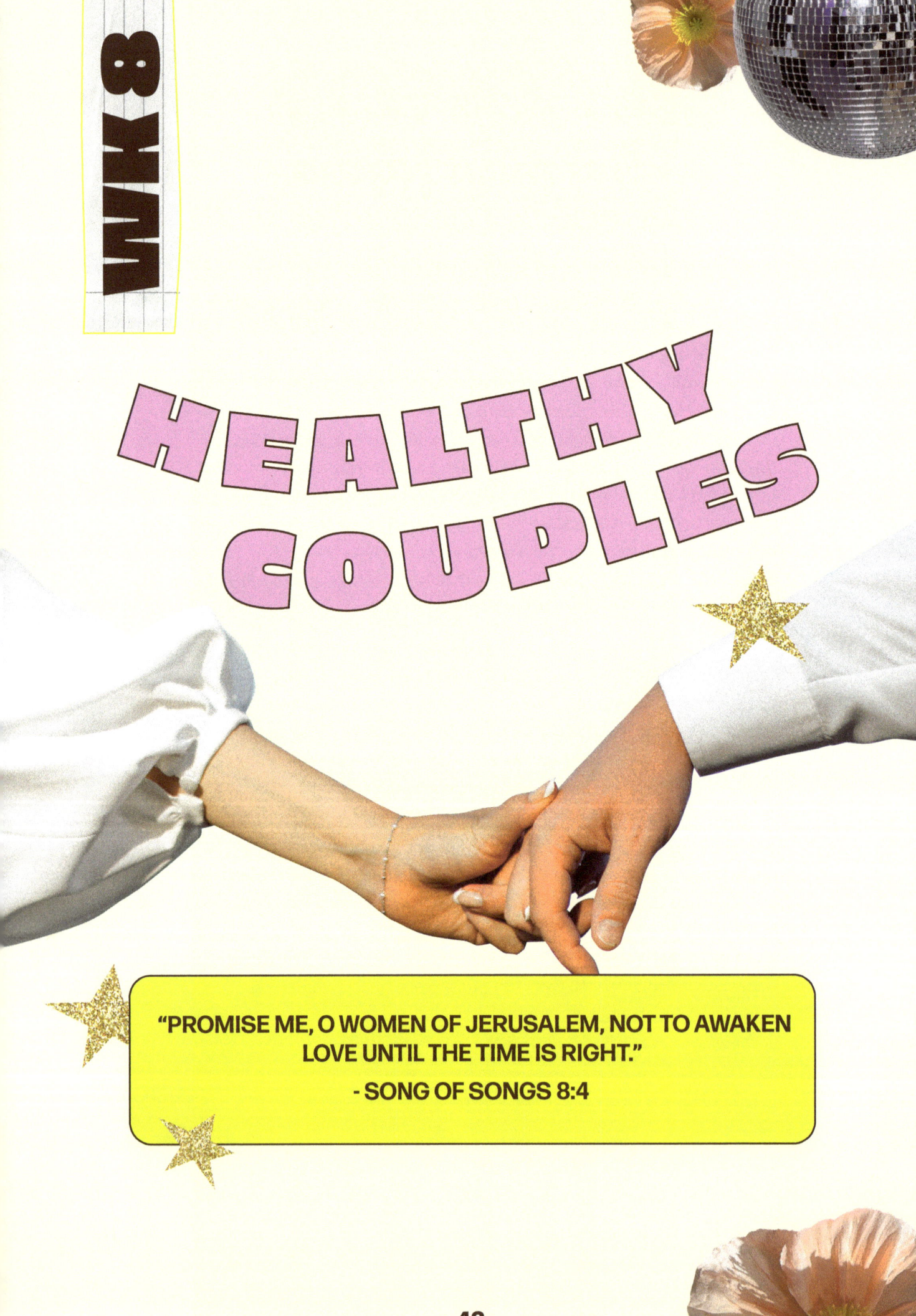

Topic Overview

WEEK 8: HEALTHY COUPLES

SERMON TITLE SUGGESTION: "Relationship Goals"

SERMON POINTS

* MATURITY MATTERS
* THE TRIANGLE TEST
* THE RIPE TIME

SCRIPTURES

* Ecclesiastes 1:1-8
* Matthew 7:16-17
* Song of Solomon 8:4

MINISTRY TIME

* Pray for God's help and guidance in the waiting season
* Pray for the Holy Spirit to align our desires to God's will
* Song: *Seasons*, Hillsong Worship, 2017[14]

CONNECT GROUP QUESTIONS

* Have you ever tried to force a circumstance before the right time? How did it turn out?
* If you were a plant, would your friends describe you as an oak tree or a seedling?
* What kind of person would you want to mother or father your future children?
* Are there any areas in your life that lack maturity and growth? [Spiritually, emotionally or physically]
* Who are your friends who will prepare you for marriage by championing your purity and growth in God?

READING FROM BREAKING UP WITH BABEL

* Chapter 7

ADDITIONAL HELPFUL RESOURCES

* *Boundaries in Dating: How Healthy Choices Grow Healthy Relationships* by Henry Cloud
* *Single, Dating, Engaged, Married: Navigating Life & Love in the Modern Age* by Ben Stuart

RELATIONSHIP GOALS
Sermon Notes

MATURITY MATTERS

A healthy Christian is someone who is physically, emotionally, spiritually and sexually healthy. This is what we call "wholeness" and something Jesus promises all of us! It's often the case that healthy people usually attract healthy people, so with this in mind, if we pursue becoming a healthy person we'll more likely attract a healthy person. Health is characterised by something that is alive, growing, fruitful and brings life to whatever is around it. The only plants that bear fruit in a garden are plants that have reached maturity, which means that if we want to have a fruitful relationship with someone, we need to be mature. By dictionary definition, the word mature means, "fully developed or ripe, completed natural growth of development, stable growth." Mature does not mean old, boring, passionless, and definitely not perfect. But there is a measure of spiritual, emotional, and physical maturity you want to look for in a partner [and ensure you've achieved personally] before attempting to grow a relationship.

PHYSICAL MATURITY

Age gaps are not as significant as you get older, but they matter in our younger years. There is no black and white principle as to when we should start dating, but there is for when we should not start. By Western law, you have to be at least eighteen to get married, which provides a good marker for us in terms of when we are mature enough. Is there any point in dating at thirteen years old when we're nowhere near the age of getting legally married? Obviously someone needs to be of physical maturity before they enter into relationships and romance, and the age for dating is getting younger and younger as preteens engage in activities far beyond their years. Song of Solomon deals with protecting the physically immature from older predators:

"What shall we do with our little sister when men come asking for her? She's a virgin and vulnerable, and we'll protect her. If they think she's a wall, we'll top it with barbed wire. If they think she's a door, we'll barricade it" [MSG].

RELATIONSHIP GOALS
Sermon Notes

EMOTIONAL MATURITY

Become [and choose] someone who is emotionally mature. How do we discern if someone is emotionally mature? Well, think about someone who is emotionally immature. They're lead by their feelings more often than their faith. They fly off the handle with a short temper. They create drama and thrive in it. You don't need to search for an emotionless robot [because that's actually another sign of emotional immaturity] but aim for someone who has grown in tempering their emotions with a good dose of faith and self control. A mature person has firm but flexible boundaries, not just for the sake of themselves but for others. Most importantly, they have integrity and the kind of character that can carry their calling.

SPIRITUAL MATURITY

Contrast a mature tree to a baby seedling. Compared to the robust strength of a mature tree, a little seedling is fresh and fragile. It needs lots of careful tending. It's too soon to tell whether it's going to last the distance and grow to maturity. Will it be scorched by the sun? Will it wither from lack of nutrition? Spiritually immature people are rarely ready to be in a relationship. They need more time to grow into a robust Christian before they leap into a relationship with someone else. A spiritually mature person is worshipping Jesus with their whole life, not just twenty-minute song segments on Sundays. Their tree has the fruit on it that brings life and benefit to those around them. We can't assess this kind of maturity on a dating profile. Time, conversation, and life experiences reveal someone's health and character. Jesus provides this good rule of thumb for identifying healthy people: Matthew 7:16–17 "You can identify them by their fruit, that is, by the way they act. Can you pick grapes from thorn- bushes, or figs from thistles? A good tree produces good fruit, and a bad tree produces bad fruit."

RELATIONSHIP GOALS
Sermon Notes

DO THE TRIANGLE TEST

Picture a triangle, with God at the top, both of you on the bottom left and right corners. As you both move UP the triangle, closer to the top [God] the closer you two become. The question is: Is the person we're pursuing an attraction or a distraction from Jesus? Is this friendship distancing me from God - or are we actually inspiring each other to lean into God more? Are you drawing closer to God as you draw closer to each other? These are important questions to honestly ask yourself when pursuing a relationship. We have a responsibility to God, and to each other, to point others toward Jesus. When we become all-consumed in "finding The One" we can miss out on fulfilling our calling in God. We mustn't substitute marriage or a relationship for the calling of God upon our life. Healthy couples protect one another's calling and personal relationship with Jesus, they don't try to take His place in their life. Be an inspiration, not a diversion!

RELATIONSHIP GOALS
Sermon Notes

THE RIPE TIME

Getting into relationship after relationship, breaking up with one person after person, results in wounding and rejection for both parties involved. It's not a great idea to build an intimate bond with someone just because it feels nice to have a hand to hold. If we don't have what it takes to honour the emotional bond we are creating, someone will wind up hurt. Let's hold our Saviour's hand until we're mature enough to hold someone else's. Song of Solomon 8:4 gives us some great relationship advice: "Oh, let me warn you, sisters in Jerusalem: Don't excite love, don't stir it up, until the time is ripe – and you're ready" [MSG].

The most important thing to remember having a fruitful relationship requires the right timing and season. If we enter into it before the right time and context it will be premature. Premature is something otherwise good that occurs before the ordained time, rendering it deformed, unhealthy, undeveloped and immature. If we force a relationship before it's due season, we can ruin it before it's ripe. Pursuing a godly relationship is not wrong, but we can do it the wrong way! When fruit is ripe to be picked, you don't have to pull it and wrench it off the vine - it yields all on its own with ease and grace, ready to be enjoyed. If your relationship is "ripe" to be picked and love ready to be "awakened" then it won't require a possessive grip, force, or haste. You'll be ready.

WK9

SEX, SCIENCE & SCRIPTURE

"DO YOU NOT KNOW THAT YOUR BODIES ARE TEMPLES OF THE HOLY SPIRIT, WHO IS IN YOU, WHOM YOU HAVE RECEIVED FROM GOD? YOU ARE NOT YOUR OWN"
- 1 CORINTHIANS 6:19

Topic Overview

WEEK 9: SEX, SCIENCE & SCRIPTURE

SERMON TITLE SUGGESTION: "The Sexual Gospel"

SERMON POINTS
* SEX IS POWERFUL
* BIOLOGY THEOLOGY
* THE POWER OF PORN
* FORGIVENESS FOR SEXUAL SIN

SCRIPTURES
* Genesis 1:28
* Ephesians 5:25-29
* 1 Corinthians 6:19

MINISTRY TIME
* Opportunity to receive forgiveness and respond in repentance
* Healing from sexual and relational brokenness
* Prayer for Holy Spirit to set people free from addictions [e.g. pornography, people, social media]
* Song suggestion: *Break Every Chain*, Will Reagan, 2012[15]

CONNECT GROUP QUESTIONS
* What are some unhelpful ways sex is presented in movies and social media?
* What are some attitudes towards sex & marriage that I might need to change?
* How is marriage defined biblically? Let's talk about why.
* How can I walk in [or continue to walk in] sexual freedom and integrity?
* Are there any areas in my life that require healing and forgiveness?

READING FROM BREAKING UP WITH BABEL
* Chapters 2, 3 & 4

ADDITIONAL HELPFUL RESOURCES
* *Teen Sex by the Book: A Call to Countercultural Living* by Patricia Weerakoon
* *Hooked: New Science on How Casual Sex is Affecting Our Children* by Joe S. McIlhaney, Jr. & Freda McKissic Bush
* *Moral Revolution: The Naked Truth About Sexual Purity* by Jason Vallotton and Kris Vallotton

THE SEXUAL GOSPEL
Sermon Notes

SEX IS POWERFUL

Sex is a wonderful gift from God! Anything God creates is inherently good, so if God came up with the idea for humans to have sex, it has to be good for us. It boosts our immune system. It gives us energy, endorphins and natural antidepressants as it bonds us intimately and permanently to our life partner. This is Genius engineering! Male and female physically fit together like a lock and key, so when their bodies join together in sexual union it unlocks fruitfulness and the potential of new life. It's amusing that people think God doesn't approve of sex when it's literally the first thing He tells humans to do: "Then God blessed them and said, 'Be fruitful and multiply" [Genesis 1:28].

This doesn't mean sex is trivial or casual. No other activity on earth is so powerful that it has the capacity to produce human life. Not even the angels are allowed the privilege of joining God in the creation of new life, since they are not sexual beings! Unless we admit that sex is powerful we tend to to misuse and abuse it - because we naturally handle powerful things differently. Fire is powerful, which means it can be both wonderful and dangerous. When we guard it within the boundaries of a fire place, it brings warmth, comfort and light to others. If left unguarded: it can burn the house down! If we don't guard our sexual habits with boundaries, it does damage not only to ourselves, but other people. But safe within the stable and permanent fireplace of marriage? It's a wonderful, life-giving thing!

THE SEXUAL GOSPEL
Sermon Notes

BIOLOGY THEOLOGY

Why is marriage the "fire place" for sex? Marriage is not a legal contract or a social construct. Spiritually speaking, it's a binding, lifelong covenant between a man and a woman. Genesis 2:24 says, "That is why a man leaves his father and mother and is united to his wife, and they become one flesh." Two can only truly become one flesh through covenant, where they vow to commit their entire lives to one another. The "forever"ness of marriage is reflected in our physiology. Sex is designed to be like superglue, sticking two people together for life. When we engage in sexual activity, powerful neurochemicals are released in our body to bond us emotionally and spiritually to our partner. Like those really strong Band Aids, this bond sticks really well the first time, but when you rip it off it takes bits of skin and hairs with it. Every time you repeat this process, more glue is removed until eventually it doesn't stick at all. This is what happens when we have sex over and over with different partners.[16]

This "glue" works differently for males and females. For women, it is primarily the hormone oxytocin, nicknamed the "love hormone" because it:

* eases stress
* creates feelings of closeness
* triggers the trust circuits in her brain
* causes her to want to nurture and protect the one she's bonded to

It's not only released in sexual activity, but oxytocin absolutely surges when a woman has a new baby to ensure she is bound to that child, and promotes a willingness to sacrifice herself for him or her.[17]

For men, the primary hormone released during sex is vasopressin. Some call it the "commitment hormone" because it:

* generates a desire for commitment to one partner
* rouses loyalty
* inspires a protective sense over one's mate

A male's brain is flooded with vasopressin during sex, creating a bond with every woman he has sexual interaction with no matter who they are. Just like oxytocin, vasopressin not only promotes bonding between sexual partners, but bonding between father and child. We're created for covenant commitment - our biology aligns with theology!

THE SEXUAL GOSPEL
Sermon Notes

THE POWER OF PORN

Sex is supposed to involve knowing and being intimately known by your covenant partner. Porn is a counterfeit of sexual blessing, providing sexual stimulation without having to honour or meet the needs of anyone else. Feeding on porn will train your brain for unrealistic sexual experiences and excessive stimulation. The dopamine hit from porn operates in a very similar way to narcotics and the excessive stimulation results in reduced capacity. Meaning, you build up a tolerance to it and need more and more to get the same result.[18] This makes for a terrible sex life! Masturbation isn't real sex - the prolactin levels released in sex is 400% higher than what is released with masturbation. What people are experiencing is a hollow release and inferior counterfeit of the real thing.

God has ordained sex to take place between a male and a female, in an exclusive, binding relationship called marriage, and He rigged the system so that it works best in that context. Ephesians 5:25-29 says, "For husbands, this means love your wives, just as Christ loved the church. He gave up his life for her...In the same way, husbands ought to love their wives as they love their own bodies." Sexual intimacy is a beautiful expression of this oneness: putting someone's needs before your own. Sex was never meant to be the giving of your self for the sake of yourself. Sexual intimacy is meant to be the yielding of your self to another in a private setting, charged with sacred mystery and trust, that results in both parties being blessed!

THE SEXUAL GOSPEL
Sermon Notes

FORGIVENESS FOR SEXUAL SIN

Paul the Apostle writes in 1 Corinthians 6:16-20, "There is a sense in which sexual sins are different from all others. In sexual sin we violate the sacredness of our own bodies, these bodies that were made for God-given and God-modelled love, for "becoming one" with another" [MSG].

Paul isn't penning this letter to either pagans or virgins. They were fresh Christians who had been swept up in a culture of sexual chaos. So he also says: "Since then, you've been cleaned up and given a fresh start by Jesus, our Master, our Messiah, and by our God present in us, the Spirit" [1 Corinthians 6:11, MSG].

These sexually broken Corinthians had given their lives to Christ and experienced his healing, forgiveness and grace! There's no room for condemnation in Scripture. Let's remember that virginity is not the same as purity; it should be the fruit of purity. It is possible to be a virgin with an impure heart. It is also possible for someone who gave away their virginity to make a Christ-led decision to repent and walk in sexual integrity once again. If you need a fresh start, you won't get it from the world, but you'll definitely get it from Jesus. Time, as it turns out, doesn't heal all wounds. No amount of minutes, meditation, or fragrant body wash will clean us up when we've stuffed it up – it's the Holy Spirit alone who carries this medicine of mercy: "God present in us". This is the [sexual] Gospel!

Topic Overview

WEEK 10: HEALING BROKENESS

SERMON TITLE SUGGESTION: "Binding Broken Hearts"

SERMON POINTS
- DAVID'S DILEMMA
- BREAKING UP WITH BAD THINKING
- METAMORPHOSIS
- RESHAPING DESIRES

SCRIPTURES
- Psalm 51:10
- Romans 12:2
- 2 Corinthians 5:17

MINISTRY TIME
- Give opportunity to surrender desires to God
- Prayer for Holy Spirit to restore purity
- Prayer for healing broken hearts
- Song Suggestion: *As You Find Me,* Hillsong United, 2019[19]

CONNECT GROUP QUESTIONS
- Have you ever changed your taste in food? [E.g. you now enjoy the taste of something you used to hate]
- Are there any patterns of thinking you need to change/turn away from in order to be transformed?
- What are some ways you could "awaken" your hunger/appetite for Jesus?
- Is there anything unhealthy in your life you need to eliminate in order to get free?
- What are some healthy ways you can move on from a break up?

READING FROM BREAKING UP WITH BABEL
- Chapters 9 & 10

ADDITIONAL HELPFUL RESOURCES
- *Gay Girl, Good God* by Jackie Hill Perry

BINDING BROKEN HEARTS
Sermon Notes

DAVID'S DILEMMA

If you thumb the pages of Israel's history, some of their greatest leaders carried the greatest brokenness, particularly in the area of relationships and sexuality. Enter King David, Israel's most beloved king. Jesus himself emerged from the blood line of David, so we naturally want David's relational track record to be squeaky clean. But most of the psalms we journal today are written from the aching corners of his heart. David was a good king and a true worshipper but he was no stranger to sexual brokenness. The opening chapters of David and Bathsheba's infamous relationship are messy and painful [2 Samuel 11]. When laziness and luxury seduced David away from fighting for the kingdom, his eyes wandered over to Bathsheba's bath time.

He took a woman who belonged to someone else and crossed about every boundary in the book to get her. David endured grief and pain because of his sin. But God, in His infinite mercy, gave him another chance to fulfil his calling. "Another chance" is the catch cry at the very heart of our gospel. And because of it, any person can sing the song of David's personal repentance while he's nursing the grave results of his own sexual sin: "Create in me a pure heart, oh God, and renew a right spirit within me" [Psalm 51:10]. No self-help book, podcast or promise ring is going to help us here. It is the power of the Spirit of God alone that restores our purity! David was no icon for virginity, but he became a beacon for purity – and whatever our past, so can we.

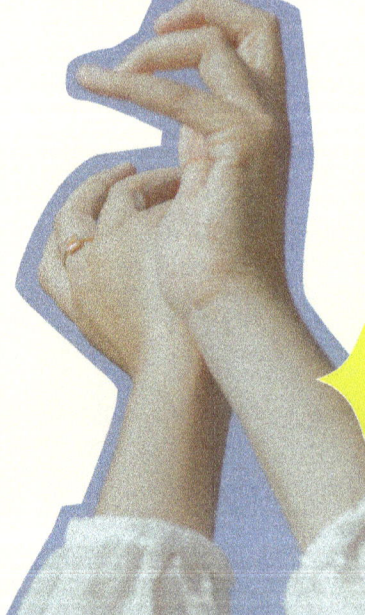

BINDING BROKEN HEARTS
Sermon Notes

BREAKING UP WITH BAD THINKING

So if we've followed in David's footsteps, how can we be healed from broken hearts and broken sexuality? The world doesn't know how. Our culture preaches a doctrine of feelings and filters to try to fix the issue of sexual brokenness. But God already gave us a part of the body that can be transformed. Ironically, it can't be seen from the outside, but it's so powerful that it tells the rest of the body what to do. Paul writes: "...be transformed by the renewing of your mind" [Romans 12:2 NIV]. If you're asking: Can I, who has experienced sexual sin and brokenness, have a meaningful and wonderful marriage, healthy sex life and fruitful future? The answer: Absolutely!

In order to experience transformation, we must change the way we think about sex, dating and relationships. Is sex merely for personal pleasure or is it an exclusive gift of intimacy for marital covenant? Is dating for selfish experimentation or is it a process of trust to discern who is appropriate to receive my gift of intimacy? Is marriage a social construct or is it a biblical covenant to reflect the mystery of the Gospel? Changing our thinking changes the neural pathways of our brain. Changing our brain changes our behaviour. And changing our behaviour changes our life.

BINDING BROKEN HEARTS
Sermon Notes

METAMORPHOSIS

If Christ can renew our mind, it means he can renew our sexual metabolisms and sexual memories, bringing us to sexual wholeness and sexual blessing. We need to confess our brokenness to God, acknowledging that the methods of the world are faulty, and God's Way is the only path to wholeness. There is no planting our feet in both camps here: we must decidedly depart from Hollywood and enter a new world through the Holy Wood of the cross.

It's time to break up with Hollywood for good and pursue the path of purity. The word for "transformation" in Romans 12:2 is metamorphoō which is where we get the English word metamorphosis. Metamorphosis isn't just "a change". We are transfigured into a creature with a new nature! When the caterpillar undergoes metamorphosis it transforms into a butterfly. It changes shape and form, becoming a new creature entering an entirely different environment with its newfound wings. It lives in the air instead of being bound to the earth. It lives on a different diet because it has a new appetite. It's why the Bible says, "...anyone who is in Christ is a new creation!" [2 Corinthians 5:17]

BINDING BROKEN HEARTS
Sermon Notes

RESHAPING OUR DESIRES

But remember, just like the butterfly endures time in the cocoon, living according to our new nature is not a one time event: it's a process! God set the Israelites free from Egyptian bondage in one night - He split the Red Sea and brought them onto resurrection ground. But then He spent 40 years feeding them flatbread from heaven - why? He was reshaping their appetites for the Promised Land, which had all the fruit, oil, wine - things they'd never dreamed of tasting and experiencing! God had to reshape their appetites in the wilderness to break their addiction to Egyptian food and start craving the things of God. Sexual wholeness requires us to starve ourselves of things that awaken an unholy appetite.

Have you noticed that whenever you watch a cooking show, it somehow awakens an appetite in you that was definitely not there when you began? You were content until you saw the brownie oozing with chocolate sauce. Suddenly, your appetite for sugar has been awakened. Even our stomachs tell us that what we look at and where we position ourselves has a big impact on our appetite and desires! If I'm trying to build healthy habits in my life when it comes to food, I won't be looking at unhealthy meals on screens or recipe books. Let's say I'm a diabetic and having certain amounts of sugar could risk my life – I may even need to hold back from socialising with people who influence me to eat junk food until I've built healthy habits and become used to my new diet.

This makes sense to us on a physical level, and we'd be wise to apply this in the area of our sexual and emotional health. The friends and community we surround ourself with is extremely important when it comes to renewing the mind and creating new habits. That includes digital community! If the eyes are the window to the soul, then social media will present us with a feast for the eyes, but it's one that can give you food poisoning. Here is the really good news about our appetites and desires: whatever appetite you feed will grow, and whatever appetite you starve will shrink. Eventually, our appetite will be reshaped and redirected toward the things that bring us life, health, wholeness and blessing. It's like drinking fresh water after realising you've been swallowing saltwater for years, wondering why you've never successfully quenched your thirst. Or feasting on fresh fruit from the Promised Land!

END NOTES

1. "Who You Say I Am" – Words and Music by Ben Fielding & Reuben Morgan © 2018 Hillsong Music and Resources LLC.

2. "No Longer Slaves" – Words and Music by Brian Johnson, Joel Case & David Helser © 2015 Bethel Music.

3. Werner Gitt, "Dazzling design in miniature: DNA information storage" Creation, 6 December 1997, https://creation.com/dazzling-design-in- miniature-dna-information-storage-creation-magazine

4. Don Batten, "Cheating With Chance", Creation.com, 27 February 2013, https://creation.com/cheating-with-chance

5. "Broken Vessels (Amazing Grace)" – Words and Music by Jonas Myrin & Joel Houston © 2014 Hillsong Music and Resources LLC.

6. "Hindsight" – Words and Music by Alexander Pappas, Aodhan King, Benjamin William Hastings & Michael Fatkin © 2018 Hillsong Music and Resources LLC.

7. Joe S. McIlhaney, Jr. & Freda McKissic Bush, *Hooked: New Science on How Casual Sex is Affecting Our Children* (Chicago, IL: Northfield publishing, 2019) 39.

8. "Build My Life" – Words and Music by Brett Younker, Karl Martin, Kirby Kaple, Matt Redman & Pat Barrett © 2018 Bowyer and Bow.

9. "Pieces" – Words and Music by Amanda Cook & Steffany Gretzinger © 2016 Bethel Music.

10. Cloud & John Townsend, *Boundaries in Dating*, 11.

END NOTES

11. Mark Gungor, *Laugh Your Way to a Better Marriage: Unlocking the Secrets to Life, Love, and Marriage* (New York, NY: Atria Paperback, 2008), 11.

12. "Promises Never Fail" – Words and Music by Ben Fielding, Brian Johnson, Jason Ingram & Joel Taylor © 2019 Bethel Music, Essential Music Publishing LLC & Hillsong Music Publishing.

13. Andy Stanley, *The New Rules for Sex, Love & Dating,* (Grand Rapids, MI: Zondervan, 2014), 27.

14. "Seasons" – Words and Music by Ben Tan, Benjamin William Hastings & Chris Davenport © 2017 Hillsong Music and Resources LLC.

15. "Break Every Chain" – Words and Music by Will Reagan © 2012 United Pursuit Records.

16. Joe S. McIlhaney, Jr. & Freda McKissic Bush, *Hooked: New Science on How Casual Sex is Affecting Our Children* (Chicago, IL: Northfield publishing, 2019) 43.

17. Matthew S. Stanford, *The Biology of Sin: Grace, Hope and Healing for Those Who Feel Trapped* (Downer's Grove, IL: InterVarsity Press, 2010), 48.

18. Patricia Weerakoon, *Teen Sex by the Book: A Call to Countercultural Living* (Sydney South, NSW: Anglican Youthworks, 2012), 169.

19. "As You Find Me" – Words and Music by Benjamin William Hastings, Joel Houston & Matt Crocker © 2019 Hillsong Music and Resources LLC.

PRAYER APPENDIX

Prayer ministry is vital to ministering around the topics we've covered in this curriculum. It's helpful to remember that prayer is not a magic incantation or formula to fix everything in a moment [although yes, sometimes we see immediate fruit if the person and moment is ripe for it.] The aim of prayer ministry is to invite Jesus into the situation so the Holy Spirit can initiate the process of transformation, illuminate areas that need healing or repentance, or bring revelation and increased understanding around an issue. These guided prayers are not for you to recite word for word as a script, but to help give you some language and direction around leading young people in a time of prayer. They're written in first person, but feel free to make it your own by inserting the name of the person into the prayer and praying it over them. They can be adapted for corporate settings after you've preached, in connect groups, or one-on-one.

FORGIVENESS:

Heavenly Father, please forgive me for my failure and rejection of you and your ways. Forgive me for doing relationships my way. I'm running to you! I'm putting my failures and mistakes at the foot of the cross. I receive your forgiveness and grace, and I thank you that your blood covers all of my sin. Holy Spirit, please illuminate areas in my heart and mind that need healing. Show me where I've gone wrong and need to turn back to you. Empower me to live a pure and powerful life, running the race for you. I pray for a new start, a new chapter, a new way of living. In Jesus' name, amen.

HEALING:

Heavenly Father, I declare you are the ultimate Healer, and I bring before you my broken heart. I bring before you all my sin, my shame, my struggles and my weakness. I ask that you would come with the healing power of your love and grace. Holy Spirit, come and soothe every sore and bind up every wound. I ask that you would break off every fear, sin, stronghold and thought that hinders me from walking in your redemption, healing and bright future you've marked out for me. In Jesus' name, amen.

HELP:

Father God, I need you! You are my strength and my protection. Right now I feel weak. I feel like I can't walk in purity and obedience, even though I know it's the only way to true life and blessing. But I believe, and I declare, that your grace is

PRAYER APPENDIX

more than enough for me. Right now I throw my weakness into your greatness. I know obedience is impossible without your Holy Spirit to help me, otherwise I'm just striving and performing. I pray that you would come with your mighty presence and power, and give me the strength I need to follow you into your good and perfect will for my life. Help me to do what is right, not just what is easy. Amen.

SURRENDER:

Jesus, I declare that you are the Lord of my life. I surrender my whole life to you. I'm giving up my feelings, my fears, my sexuality, my thoughts and my desires - and I'm handing them all over to you. I choose you, and I let go of anything that you don't want me to hold onto. Show me what you want me to release. Give me a humble heart and help me to trust you even if your way is not what I want to choose right now. I believe you are a good God and would never ask me to give up something unless it was good for me to do so. Amen.

REVELATION:

Lord thankyou that you have sent your Spirit to open my eyes and lead me into the truth. I pray that you would reveal to me the truth about this topic, and help me to understand your heart. Your ways are higher and better, and I pray that you would help me to see your ways for my own life. I pray that all this information and teaching I have received would become revelation - that it would be planted like a seed in my heart that would grow and produce fruit for your Kingdom. In Jesus' name, Amen.

THE FUTURE:

Heavenly Father, thankyou so much for the bright future you've prepared for me! Thankyou that you see me, know me, love me and have called me by name. Lord, would you help me to walk this journey well? Would you give me the wisdom for the season I'm in and the seasons to come? Lord, provide me with friends who will encourage me and chase after you. Help me to serve my friends and help them grow into all you've called them to be. Lord, I trust you. I commit all my relationships to you. Amen.

RECOMMENDED RESOURCES

Dent, Nikki. *Breaking Up with Babel: The Gospel of Sex, Dating and Relating in a Culture of Confusion.* Brisbane, QLD: BUWB Books, 2023.

Creation Ministries International: https://creation.com

Vallotton, Jason and K. Vallotton. *Moral Revolution: The Naked Truth About Sexual Purity.* South Bloomington, MN: Chosen Books, 2014.

Weerakoon, Patricia. *Teen Sex by the Book: A Call to Countercultural Living.* Sydney South, NSW: Anglican Youthworks, 2012.

Branch, Dr. J. Alan. *Affirming God's Image: Addressing the Transgender Question with Science and Scripture.* Bellingham, WA: Lexham Press, 2019.

Branch, Dr. J. Alan. *Born This Way?: Homosexuality, Science, and the Scriptures.* Bellingham, WA: Lexham Press, 2016.

James, Sharon. *Gender Ideology: What Do Christians Need to Know.* Fearn, Ross-shire: Christian Focus Publications Ltd, 2019.

Morgan, Hillary and A. Davidson. *Mama Bear Apologetics Guide to Sexuality: Empowering Your Kids to Understanding and Live Out God's Design.* Eugene, OR: Harvest House Publishers, 2021.

Gungor, Mark. *Laugh Your Way to a Better Marriage: Unlocking the Secrets to Life, Love, and Marriage.* New York, NY: Atria Paperback, 2008.

Childers, Alisa. *Another Gospel?: A Lifelong Christian Seeks Truth in

RECOMMENDED RESOURCES

Response to Progressive Christianity. Carol Stream, IL: Tyndale Publishers, 2020.

Stuart, Ben. *Single, Dating, Engaged, Married: Navigating Life & Love in the Modern Age.* Nashville, TN: HarperCollins Publishers, 2017.

Stanley, Andy. *The New Rules for Sex, Love and Dating.* Grand Rapids, MI: Zondervan, 2014.

Perry, Jackie Hill. *Gay Girl, Good God: The Story of Who I Was and Who God Has Always Been.* Nashville, TN: B&H Publishing Group, 2018.

Smith, Judah. *Dating Delilah: Purity from a New Perspective.* Kirkland, WA: The City Church.

about the author

Nikki Dent is a pastor, Bible teacher, and itinerant preacher who lives with her husband and three daughters on the East Coast of Australia. She has passionately taught on sex, dating, and relationships from a Christian worldview for ten years in Christian leadership academies, discipleship training schools, churches and young adult ministries. Nikki is an ordained pastor with the ACC [Australian Christian Churches] and believes teaching on biblical sexuality is crucial for all expressions of the Church.

Nikki has recently published her book *Breaking Up with Babel: The Gospel of Sex, Dating, and Relating in a Culture of Confusion.* In it she explores the powerful and positive theology [and biology] of sex, dating & romance, in a way that compels Christians to walk in purity, passion and hope for SO much more than what Hollywood humanism offers us! Find the biblical answers you need on topics such as:

* How does sex affect my body, soul and spirit?
* Why should I wait until marriage to have sex?
* Why is pornography terrible for my sex life?
* How do I date biblically in a digital world?
* What kind of boundaries are helpful for healthy relationships?
* How can I be restored from heartache and brokenness?

Breaking Up with Babel is your guide to growing wholesome relationships that outshine the humanistic messages of broken sexuality. Get your copy today!

Head to: www.breakingupwithbabel.com for book purchases and speaking requests

Follow: @nikkident_ on Instagram to stay in touch

Email: hello@breakingupwithbabel.com for contact and inquiries

www.ingramcontent.com/pod-product-compliance
Lightning Source LLC
Chambersburg PA
CBHW041713290426
44109CB00029B/2864